T0036557

THE SPECTACULAR SCIENCE OF
THE LIVING WORLD

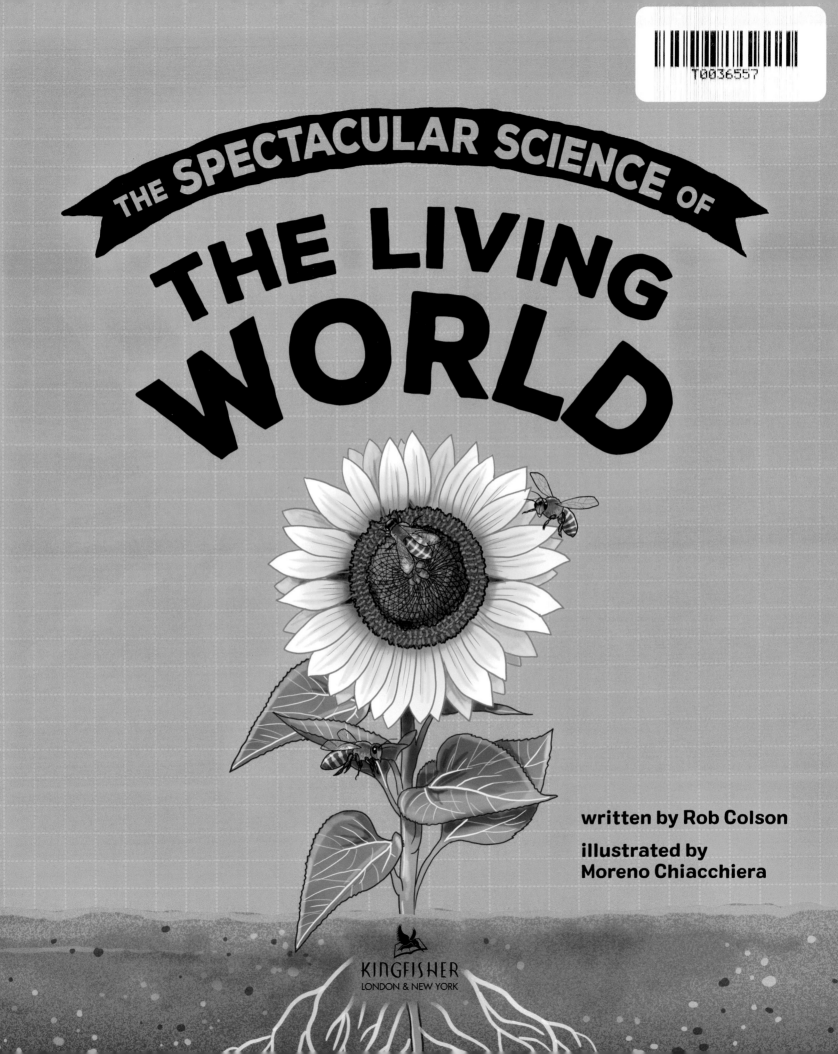

written by Rob Colson

illustrated by
Moreno Chiacchiera

KINGFISHER
LONDON & NEW YORK

KINGFISHER
LONDON & NEW YORK

First published 2024 in the United States
by Kingfisher
120 Broadway, New York, NY 10271
Kingfisher is an imprint of
Macmillan Children's Books, London
All rights reserved.

Copyright © Macmillan Publishers
International Ltd 2024

ISBN 978-0-7534-7964-3

Distributed in the U.S. and Canada by
Macmillan, 120 Broadway, New York, NY 10271

Library of Congress Cataloging-in-
Publication data has been applied for.

Author: Rob Colson
Illustrator: Moreno Chiacchiera
Consultant: Dr Nick Crumpton
Designed and edited by Tall Tree Ltd

Kingfisher Books are available for special
promotions and premiums.
For details contact:
Special Markets Department, Macmillan
120 Broadway, New York, NY 10271.

For more information please visit:
www.kingfisherbooks.com

Printed in China
2 4 6 8 9 7 5 3 1
1TR/1223/WKT/RV/128MA

EU representative: 1st Floor, The Liffey Trust
Centre 117-126 Sheriff Street Upper,
Dublin 1 D01 YC43A

FSC
www.fsc.org

MIX
Paper | Supporting
responsible forestry
FSC® C116313

CONTENTS

LIFE ON EARTH

Earth is the only place in the Universe where we know there is life. The huge variety of life forms found on our planet all have a single common ancestor, which lived around 4 billion years ago. Different species have arisen since then through a process called evolution.

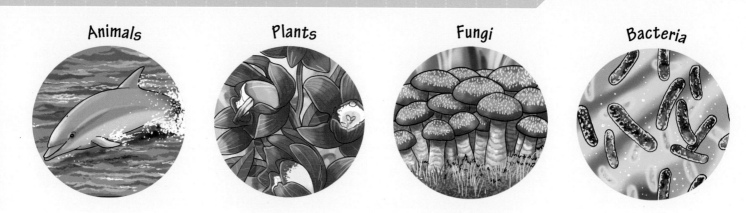

Animals   Plants   Fungi   Bacteria

LIVING ORGANISMS

Living organisms are made up of one or more cells. They come in a wide range of forms, from huge animals made of trillions of cells to tiny single-cell bacteria that are too small to see with the naked eye. Organisms are able to feed and maintain themselves so that they can grow and reproduce.

What is a species?

A species is a population of organisms that are very closely related to one another. Each species is adapted to live in a niche. A species' niche is the role it plays in the places where it lives, or habitats, such as the food it eats or the food it provides for other species. Some species can live in a wide variety of places, while others occupy a niche in just one kind of place. For example, the koala only feeds on the leaves of eucalyptus trees in Australia.

CHARLES DARWIN

English naturalist Charles Darwin (1809–1882) outlined his theory of evolution by natural selection in his book *On the Origin of Species* (1859). Along with fellow naturalist Alfred Russel Wallace, Darwin proposed that new species evolve through gradual change over many generations. Offspring are born with slight variations, and the offspring that are best adapted to their environment survive and reproduce. In this way, species change over time as their environment changes. Evidence from fossils, anatomy, and genetics has since confirmed that Darwin and Wallace's theory is correct.

CLADISTICS

Cladistics is a way of constructing diagrams to show evolutionary family trees. The branches of the tree trace today's species back to a species in the past that is their most recent common ancestor. For example, humans and chimpanzees share a common ancestor that lived about 6 million years ago. A group of species that share the same common ancestor is called a clade. Scientists create graphs called cladograms showing these relationships.

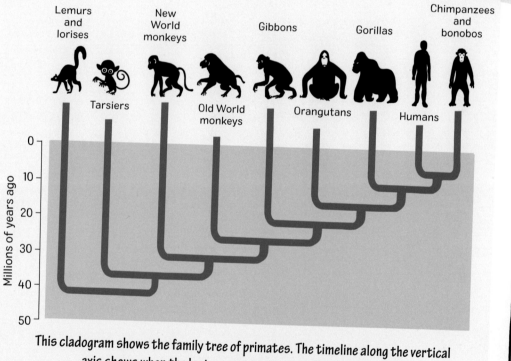

This cladogram shows the family tree of primates. The timeline along the vertical axis shows when the last common ancestor of each group lived.

The search for LUCA

Darwin suggested that all living organisms are descended from a last universal common ancestor, or LUCA. Evidence from genetics supports Darwin's idea. Scientists think that LUCA lived about 4 billion years ago. We do not know where it lived, but it may have been a single-celled organism taking energy from deep-sea hydrothermal vents.

BIOMES AND ECOSYSTEMS

Plants, animals, and other organisms live together in areas called biomes. The lives of the organisms within a biome are connected to one another as part of an ecosystem.

BIOMES

A biome is a place where a particular group of organisms live. The plants and animals that live in a biome need to be well adapted to the conditions found there, such as the temperature or rainfall. There are many biomes on Earth. These are some of the most important biomes.

1. Tundra
Tundra is found in cold regions near the poles. Covered in snow during winter, the tundra comes to life in spring when the snow melts and a range of small plants come into flower.

2. Desert
Desert biomes are found in areas of land with very little rainfall. They vary from the baking hot Sahara Desert to the freezing cold Antarctica. Life in deserts is hard, and organisms need to be specially adapted to the lack of water. Cacti have deep roots to reach underground water, thick stems to store water, and spiny leaves to minimize water loss.

3. Aquatic
Aquatic biomes are found in the seas and oceans, lakes, rivers, and marshlands. Fish are adapted to a life spent entirely under water. They breathe by taking in oxygen dissolved in the water through their gills.

ECOSYSTEMS

A community of different organisms living together in a biome forms an ecosystem. The animals, plants, and microorganisms of an ecosystem are all connected to one another. For example, plants take energy from the Sun and are then eaten by animals. Those animals are food for other animals. These relationships can be shown by drawing a food web such as the one to the right. If you take out any of the links in the food web, the whole ecosystem can suffer.

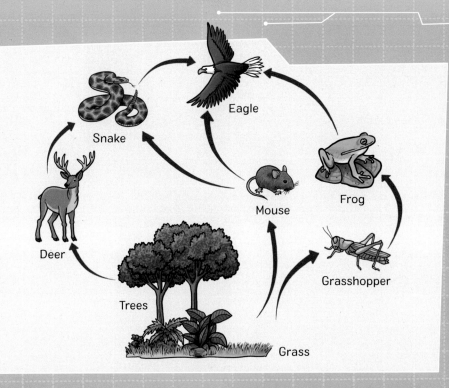

Snake

Eagle

Frog

Mouse

Deer

Grasshopper

Trees

Grass

4. Grasslands
Grasslands are areas with few trees that are dominated by grasses. The grasses are food to a variety of large mammals, such as bison, which have specially adapted stomachs to digest the tough plants.

5. Forest
Forest biomes are areas dominated by trees. They cover one-third of the land on Earth and are home to diverse groups of organisms. The trees are connected to one another by a complex underground system of roots and fungi (see page 10).

6. Polar
Polar biomes are found near the North and South Poles. Very little life can survive on land near the poles, but the cold oceans are rich in small crustaceans called krill, which are food to large animals such as humpback whales.

One humpback whale can eat 2 tons of krill in a single day.

PLANTS

Plants form the foundation of much of life on Earth. They make their own food using the energy of the Sun. In this way, they provide energy to all the organisms that eat them.

PHOTOSYNTHESIS

Plants capture the energy of the Sun in a process called photosynthesis. Photosynthesis takes place inside plant cells using a chemical called chlorophyll. Chlorophyll reflects green light but absorbs all other colors. Plants use the energy absorbed by the chlorophyll to combine carbon dioxide from the air with water to make sugars. This process releases oxygen into the air.

Light energy

Oxygen

Carbon dioxide

Sugar

Minerals

Water

POLLINATION

Flowering plants reproduce sexually (see page 32). The flowers have both male and female parts. The male sperm need to find a way to the female reproductive parts. This is called pollination. Some plants can pollinate themselves, but most plants need to be pollinated by sperm from other plants.

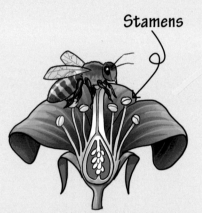

Stamens

The sperm is contained in a powdery substance called pollen, which is produced by the flower's stamens.

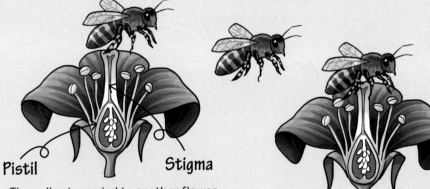

Pistil   **Stigma**

The pollen is carried to another flower, either by the wind or an animal, where it is deposited on the stigma, the receptive tip of the pistil, which is the female reproductive part of a flower.

A bee can visit up to 1,500 flowers in a single day. Its body may be covered with the pollen from dozens of different species of plant.

Many plants produce a sweet liquid called nectar to attract animals such as bees. They advertise themselves with brightly colored petals. While the animals drink the nectar, pollen is deposited on their bodies to be carried to the next flower.

Specialist feeders

The sword-billed hummingbird is a specialist feeder. It uses its 5-inch-long beak to reach the nectar at the bottom of plants with long, tubelike flowers, which other animals cannot reach. This is an example of co-evolution, in which the animal and plant species have evolved together for their mutual benefit.

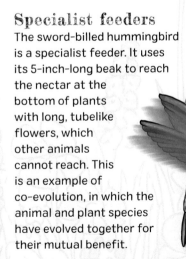

WOOD WIDE WEB

The trees and plants in a forest communicate with each other by sending chemicals along underground networks of roots, fungi, and bacteria. This network has been called the Wood Wide Web.

Fungal network

The networks are formed by a combination of roots and fungi. Fungi send out tubes called hyphae through the soil. The hyphae weave into the tips of plant roots to make a structure called a mycorrhiza. The mycorrhizas connect the trees and plants in the forest to one another.

Hyphae

Root

A mushroom is a fruiting body that a fungus grows in order to reproduce.

Symbiosis

The plants and fungi in a wood live together in symbiosis. This means that they both benefit from the other's presence. The fungi take food from the roots, absorbing sugars that trees make through photosynthesis (see page 8). The plants receive nutrients such as phosphorus and nitrogen that the fungi have taken from the soil.

Early warning system

Plants use the mycorrhizal networks to distribute resources, and young seedlings receive nutrients from larger trees via the network. The plants also use the network to communicate with one another. A plant under attack by aphids can send out a warning across the network that triggers nearby plants to put in place chemical defenses to stop the aphids from feeding on their sap.

Mother tree

SUZANNE SIMARD

The idea of the Wood Wide Web was developed by Canadian ecologist Suzanne Simard (born 1960) while she was working for a logging company in the forests of British Columbia. Simard identified large trees that she called the "mother trees," which act as central hubs for the mycorrhizal networks. The mother trees infect seedlings around them with fungi to connect them to the network. Simard's work helps conservationists to maintain forests by showing how trees cooperate with one another.

ANIMALS

While plants make their own food, animals need to eat other organisms for their energy. Some animals are simple creatures, but others have evolved amazing complexity that allows them to move around, find food, and avoid being eaten themselves!

VERTEBRATES

Vertebrates are animals with a backbone, or spine. They have a brain enclosed by a skull. Nerves from the brain run down the spine, protected by the bones. Most large animals are vertebrates. These include fish, mammals, reptiles, amphibians, and birds.

Mammals   Fish   Birds   Reptiles

INVERTEBRATES

Invertebrates are animals that do not have a backbone or bony skeleton. More than 95 percent of all animal species are invertebrates. They range from tiny mites to huge squid with eyes the size of basketballs.

Spiders and mites   Mollusks   Insects   Millipedes

Cold- or warm-blooded?
Amphibians and reptiles are often called "cold-blooded." In fact, their blood can get very warm, but they lack the ability to maintain a constant temperature. In cold weather, their blood cools and they can become lethargic. Mammals and birds are called "warm-blooded" because they keep their bodies at the same temperature regardless of the weather. They have to eat a lot of food to keep their bodies at higher temperatures than their surroundings.

Fish

Fish are vertebrates that live in water. There are about 20,000 species of fish, most of which are found in the world's oceans. Many small fish swim together in huge shoals. Atlantic herring sometimes come together to form megashoals made up of hundreds of millions of individuals. Swimming in large groups helps to protect the individual fish from being eaten by predators.

CARL LINNAEUS

Swedish biologist Carl Linnaeus (1707–1778) created the system for naming species that we use today. Each species has a two-part scientific name. The first part of the name gives the genus, while the second part gives the species. A genus is a small group of closely related species. For example, the lion's scientific name is *Panthera leo*. The genus *Panthera* also includes tigers, jaguars, and leopards. Each time a new species is discovered, it is placed in a genus and given a unique second name.

Mollusks

Mollusks are invertebrates with soft bodies that are often protected by a hard shell. They include snails, clams, cuttlefish, and octopuses.

Cuttlefish can change the color and texture of their skin in less than one second. They use this ability to camouflage themselves against the ocean floor. They also use color to communicate with one another. A courting male may display a pulsating zebra-stripe pattern on one side of its body to attract a female, while displaying typically female coloring on the other side to fool other males into thinking he is female.

Scientists think that the wide "W"-shaped pupil of a cuttlefish's eye may help it to see color.

BIRDS

Birds are animals with feathered wings. Most birds are able to fly. They are superbly adapted to life in the air, and some can fly all the way around the world.

MIGRATION

Many birds migrate from one part of the world to another each year.

Large birds such as Canada geese (right) migrate in family groups. The geese breed during the summer in northern areas. When the young are strong enough to fly, the whole family flies south for the winter.

The Arctic tern (below) has the longest migration of any bird. Each year, it flies from the Arctic Circle to the Antarctic Circle and back again. An Arctic tern can live for more than 30 years. By the end of its life, it may have flown as far as 1.6 million miles—that's the distance from Earth to the Moon and back three times!

HOW DO BIRDS FLY?

Birds fly by flapping their wings up and down to create an upward force called lift and a forward force called thrust.

Long, stiff flight feathers give the wings a large surface area to maximize lift and thrust.

Birds have very strong breast muscles to power their wings.

To make their bodies as light as possible, birds' bones are hollow, with thin, crisscrossing struts to give them strength.

Flightless birds

Some birds have lost their ability to fly through evolution. Penguins use their wings like flippers to help them to swim. Ostriches (below) have powerful legs and can run at up to 40 mph. They have relatively small wings, which they stretch out to help keep their balance as they run.

Families of geese will often fly in a "V" formation. The birds behind the lead bird benefit from decreased wind resistance. The geese take turns doing the hard work of flying at the front.

Living dinosaurs

Birds are the only animals alive today with dinosaur ancestors. In 2013, a fossilized birdlike dinosaur called *Aurornis* was discovered in China. It lived 160 million years ago and may be a direct ancestor of modern birds. Unlike today's birds, it had teeth and clawed wings.

MAMMALS

Mammals are a group of animals whose young are nourished by their mother's milk. Mammals produce smaller numbers of young than most reptiles and amphibians and give them large amounts of care.

Finger bone

Membrane

PLACENTAL MAMMALS

Placental mammals are a group of mammals whose young develop inside their mothers, nourished by a placenta. This is a diverse group of mammals that includes tiny bats and shrews, and huge elephants and whales.

Bats are the only mammals that can fly. Their wings are modified forearms with elongated fingers. A thin membrane of skin is attached to the fingers.

Brazilian free-tailed bat

The Brazilian free-tailed bat can fly horizontally at up to 100 mph. This may make them the fastest flying animals of all, speedier than any bird. In 2016, scientists measured the bats' speeds by fitting them with radio transmitters and tracking their movements.

RODENTS

Nearly half of all mammal species are rodents. All rodents have a pair of continuously growing front teeth that they use to gnaw.

The naked mole rat of East Africa (right) is a rodent that spends its whole life underground. Family groups of naked mole rats live together in complex systems of underground tunnels, which they dig out with their teeth.

MARSUPIALS

Marsupials give birth to tiny young, which grow inside their mother's pouch. The red kangaroo is the largest marsupial in the world. Males can reach 6 feet tall. The kangaroos hop around at up to 40 mph. They can leap 30 feet in a single hop. Key to their powerful leaps are the stretchy tendons that run along the backs of their hind legs. The tendons turn their legs into springs, providing the energy to propel them into the air.

MONOTREMES

Monotremes are mammals that lay eggs. The platypus is a monotreme that lives in Australia. It forages for small invertebrates in freshwater streams. When it dives, a platypus closes its eyes, ears, and nostrils. It relies on its sensitive bill to find its prey. The bill is packed with sensors and can detect the weak electrical charges given off by living bodies.

Large thigh muscles

Thick, stretchy Achilles tendon

Long feet

Life in the water

Cetaceans are mammals that live their whole lives in the water. They include whales, dolphins, and porpoises. Weighing up to 150 tons, the blue whale is the largest animal that has ever lived!

MAASAI MARA

The Maasai Mara is a national park in southern Kenya, Africa. Its open grasslands are home to a wide variety of grazing animals, including 1.5 million wildebeest and 400,000 zebras. These large grazers are hunted by a number of fierce predators.

UMBRELLA TREE

The most common tree in the Maasai Mara is the acacia, or umbrella tree. Acacia leaves are a favorite meal for giraffes. They use their 20-inch-long tongue to reach through the sharp thorns and pull off the leaves.

ANCIENT TREES

The African baobab tree survives the long dry season by storing water in its wide trunk, which can reach a diameter of more than 30 feet. Baobabs live for a very long time. A tree in Zimbabwe was 2,450 years old when it died in 2011.

During the dry season, elephants strip the bark off baobab trees with their tusks. This allows them access to water stored in the inner part of the tree.

MIGRATING WILDEBEEST

More than 1 million wildebeest migrate across the Maasai Mara each year, following the seasonal rains. Danger awaits them when they cross the River Mara. Nile crocodiles patrol the waters on the lookout for any animal that is struggling. The crocodiles often team up to grab hold of a wildebeest by the neck and hold its head under the water to drown it.

Secretary birds are birds of prey that hunt on foot. They roam the open grasslands and eat a wide range of animals, including lizards, snakes, and scorpions. They kill their prey by stomping on them.

Lazing lions

Lions are the only big cats that live together in large groups, which are called prides. A typical pride contains about six or seven adult females and their cubs plus two or three adult males. Lions spend much of the day sleeping and do most of their hunting at night, when their excellent night vision gives them an advantage over their prey.

AMPHIBIANS

Amphibians are animals that start their lives in water before undergoing large changes to their bodies that allow many of them to emerge onto land.

METAMORPHOSIS

As they grow up, amphibians such as frogs undergo an extraordinary transformation, called metamorphosis.

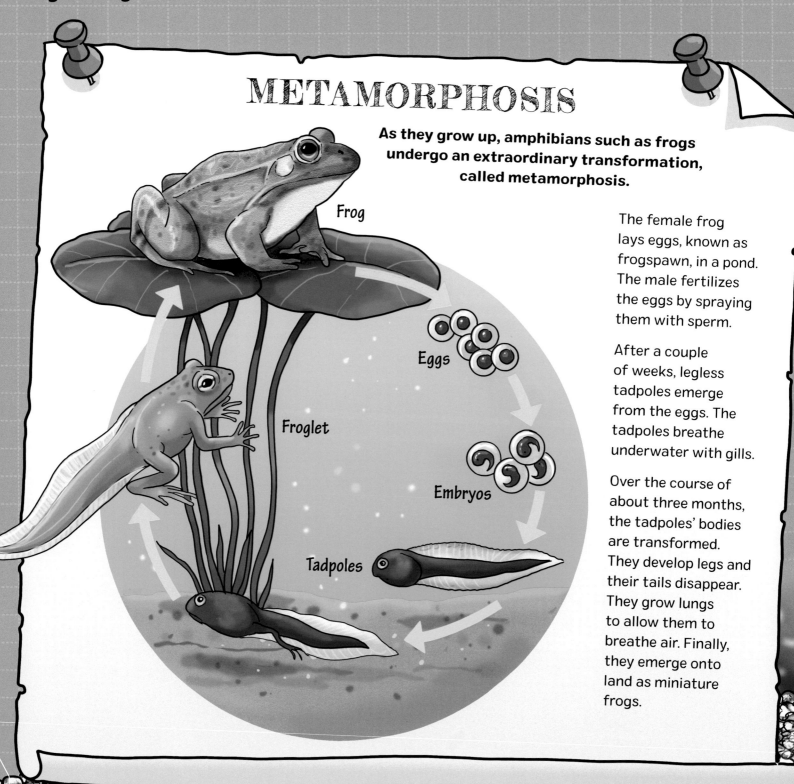

Frog

Froglet

Eggs

Embryos

Tadpoles

The female frog lays eggs, known as frogspawn, in a pond. The male fertilizes the eggs by spraying them with sperm.

After a couple of weeks, legless tadpoles emerge from the eggs. The tadpoles breathe underwater with gills.

Over the course of about three months, the tadpoles' bodies are transformed. They develop legs and their tails disappear. They grow lungs to allow them to breathe air. Finally, they emerge onto land as miniature frogs.

SALAMANDERS

Like all amphibians, salamanders lay their eggs in water. Some salamanders remain in water for their whole lives, while others crawl out of the water as adults.

Growing up to 6 feet long, the Chinese giant salamander is the world's largest amphibian. It lives in small streams, feeding on a wide range of prey, including fish, crabs, and other amphibians. It has very poor eyesight but can sense tiny vibrations in the water that indicate the presence of prey.

The axolotl, which lives in lakes in central Mexico, is a salamander that never grows up. It spends its entire life at a larval stage, breathing in the water with its featherlike gills.

Caecilians

Caecilians are snakelike amphibians that live hidden in the soil in tropical regions, feeding on earthworms. They spend their entire lives underground.

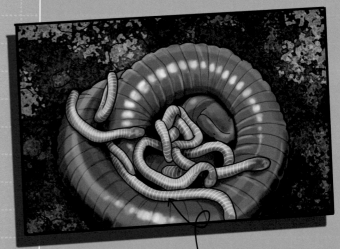

Some baby caecilians feed on their mother's skin.

Axolotl

6 feet

Chinese giant salamander

REPTILES

Like amphibians, reptiles lay eggs. The eggs are leathery and waterproof, which allows reptiles to lay their eggs away from water. A reptile's skin is dry and covered in scales or plates.

TURTLES

Green turtles range across tropical oceans. They spend almost their whole lives at sea, but the females must come to land to lay their eggs. They return to the beach where they hatched themselves and lay about 100 eggs, which they bury in the sand. The baby turtles hatch during the night about two months later and head straight for the ocean. This is the most dangerous time in their lives, and many hatchlings are picked off on the beach by predators such as gulls.

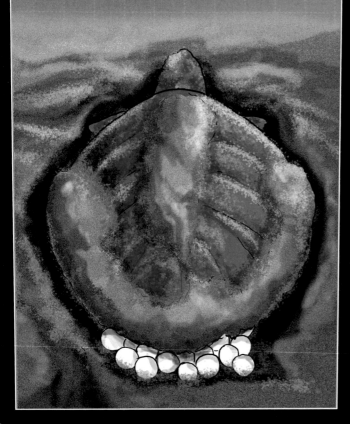

SLITHERING SNAKES

Snakes are a group of reptiles that have lost their legs. They move using their whole bodies, which are flexible and muscular. Snakes can move in four different ways.

Rectilinear
The snake pulls itself forward with a series of contractions of its muscles. Large snakes often move this way.

Serpentine
The snake moves forward using a series of horizontal waves. Snakes also swim this way.

Concertina
The snake moves its front half forward and coils it, then pulls its back half forward. It then coils its back half and pushes its front half forward. Snakes often climb trees like this.

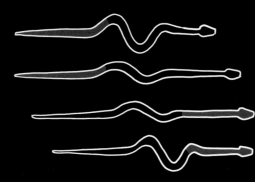

Sidewinding
The snake successively lifts different parts of its body off the ground and moves them sideways. Snakes sidewind when moving across sand.

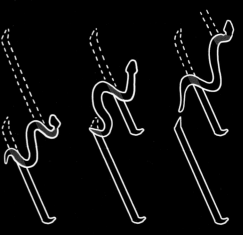

CROCS

Crocodilians are large reptiles that mostly hunt in the water. They are more closely related to birds and dinosaurs than to other reptiles!

With just their eyes and nostrils showing above the water, crocodiles can approach prey unnoticed.

Measuring up to 16 feet long, the saltwater crocodile is the largest living crocodilian. It patrols coastal wetlands and mangrove swamps and will attack almost anything that enters its territory, including sharks.

The American alligator is native to the southern states of the USA. It is the top predator in marshes and swamps, feeding on anything it can catch.

The gharial is a specialist fish-eater. It lives in rivers in India and uses its thin snout to catch its prey. The snout detects vibrations in the water. It whips the snout from side to side to zero in on fish and grabs them with its powerful jaw, which is lined with more than 100 teeth.

AMAZON RAIN FOREST

Howler monkeys

Amazon rain forest

BRAZIL

Amazon river

PERU

The dense Amazon rain forest makes up about half of all the rain forest in the world. It spreads across the Amazon basin in South America, which is the drainage basin of the Amazon River and its tributaries.

The mighty Amazon

The Amazon River rises in the Andes Mountains in Peru, and flows east for 4,000 miles to empty into the Atlantic Ocean in Brazil. Along the way, the river swells to an enormous size, and it is 120 miles wide when it reaches the ocean. About one-sixth of the world's fresh water that drains into the oceans flows through the mouth of the Amazon.

Amazon river dolphin

Jaguar

Poison-dart frog

CARLOS NOBRE

Brazilian climate scientist Carlos Nobre (born 1951) works to reverse the destruction of the Amazon rain forest. He argues that areas that have been cleared need to be changed back into forest in order to help in the fight against climate change. If we do not do this, Nobre fears that the whole forest could be lost.

There are about **400 billion** trees in the Amazon rain forest.

AMAZON WILDLIFE

Poison-dart frogs are brightly colored as a warning to other animals to leave them alone. The frogs have poisonous skin that will kill most potential predators.

Howler monkeys are one of the loudest land animals on Earth. From high in the trees, they howl at one another at dawn and at dusk. Their cries are as loud as a gunshot and can be heard up to 3 miles away.

Jaguars are large cats with an exceptionally powerful bite. Unlike most cats, which bite the neck to kill their prey, jaguars bite right through the skull. Most jaguars have reddish-yellow coats with black spots, which help to keep them camouflaged, but about 10 percent of jaguars have jet black coats. These are known as black panthers.

Green anacondas are the heaviest snake in the world, weighing up to 150 pounds. The anaconda spends most of its life in the water, waiting for unsuspecting prey to stop for a drink. It kills its prey by wrapping its body around them and squeezing them to death. Anacondas can go for months between meals if they catch a large animal such as a tapir or a deer.

Amazon river dolphins find their way around the muddy waters of the rivers using echolocation. They give off a series of rapid clicks and listen out for the echo bouncing back off prey such as a catfish. The melon at the front of the dolphin's head is a mass of fatty tissue that focuses the sounds it makes during echolocation.

Mackaw

Toucan

Green anaconda

Melon

Echoes bounce back off prey.

Tapir

25

INSECTS AND ARACHNIDS

Insects are invertebrates with a body divided into three parts and six legs. Scientists have identified about 1 million species of insect, and there are many more left to be discovered.

BATTLING BEETLES

Nearly half of all known insect species are beetles. These insects have tough exoskeletons, which take a huge variety of shapes. The male Hercules beetle is the longest beetle in the world. It can measure up to 6.5 inches long. The males use their long horns to fight one another.

Hercules beetles

Insect architects

Termites are small insects that live in large colonies of up to 1 million individuals. They build mounds with sophisticated ventilation systems. The termites farm fungus inside the mounds to feed to their young.

Night

Morning

Midday

Afternoon

Architects study the way air flows through termite mounds to find ways to improve the efficiency of skyscraper ventilation.

ARACHNIDS

Arachnids are invertebrates with eight legs. They include spiders, mites and scorpions.

12 in

GOLIATH BIRDEATER

The largest spider in the world is the Goliath birdeater, which grows up to 12 inches long. Despite its name, it rarely catches birds. It feeds on insects, frogs, lizards, and small rodents.

Scorpions

The front legs of a scorpion form a pair of grasping pincers. Its tail ends in a venomous stinger, which it uses to kill its prey. Female scorpions carry their young on their backs while their exoskeletons harden.

Stinger   Pincers

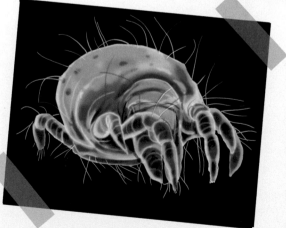

Dust mites are tiny eyeless arachnids just 0.02 inch long. They feed on dead skin cells.

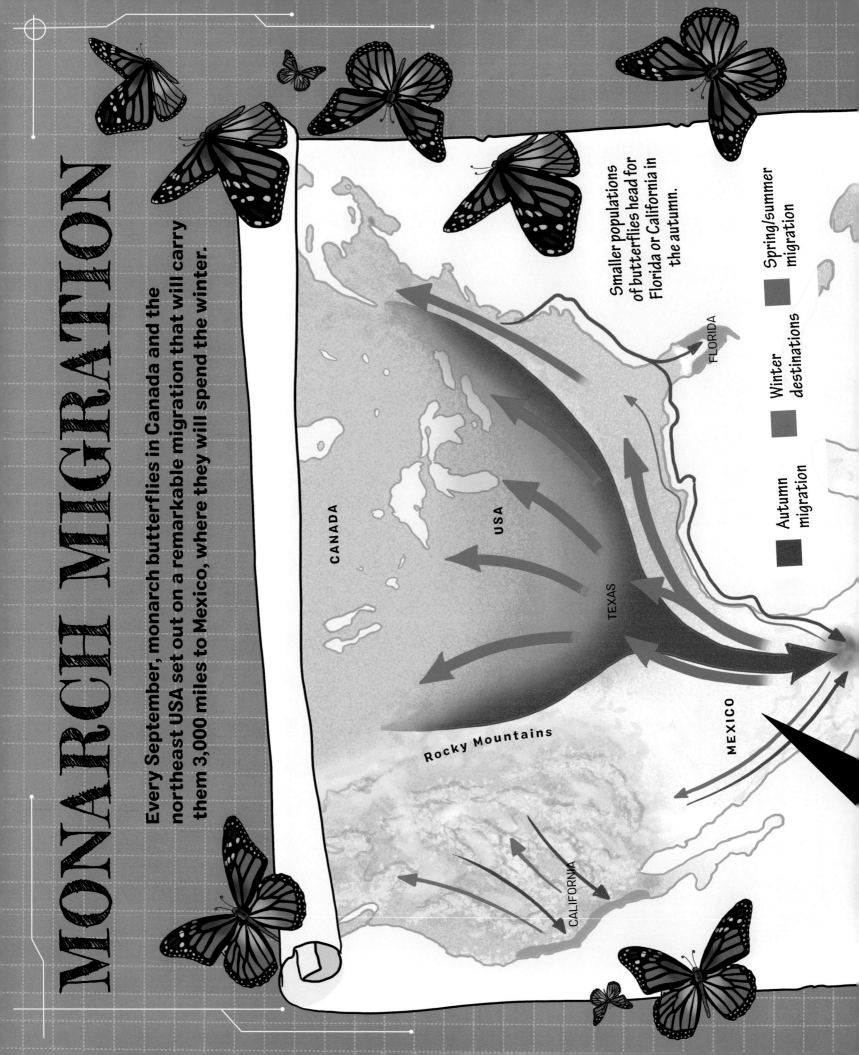

MONARCH MIGRATION

Every September, monarch butterflies in Canada and the northeast USA set out on a remarkable migration that will carry them 3,000 miles to Mexico, where they will spend the winter.

Smaller populations of butterflies head for Florida or California in the autumn.

CANADA

USA

Rocky Mountains

TEXAS

FLORIDA

MEXICO

CALIFORNIA

Autumn migration

Winter destinations

Spring/summer migration

Southbound

Weighing just half a gram—lighter than a paper clip—the butterflies take advantage of air currents to carry them south, completing the journey in under two months. Their destination is the oyamel fir forests that grow on mountainsides in central Mexico. When they reach the forests, the monarchs cluster together to stay warm. Tens of thousands of insects may shelter in a single tree. They will remain there until spring.

Returning north

In spring, the butterflies head back north, but these individuals will not complete the journey. When they reach warmer places, such as Texas, the butterflies mate and lay their eggs in milkweed plants. This first generation of butterflies then dies.

The caterpillars feed on the milkweed before transforming into adults and flying a few hundred miles farther north to find a new patch of milkweed on which to lay eggs. Each generation of monarchs in the summer lives for just a few weeks. In this way, the butterflies work their way back to their starting point.

The individuals that make the next year's epic migration are on average the great-great-grandchildren of the monarchs that flew south the previous year!

Pollinators

As they pass through North America, the monarch butterflies play an important role as pollinators. The adult butterflies visit many different flowers in search of nectar. In doing so, they transfer pollen from one plant to another.

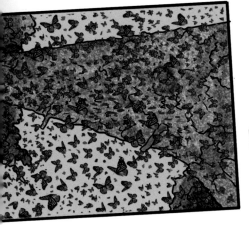

Navigating by the Sun

The monarch butterflies use the Sun to navigate during their long migration. To do this, they need to keep track of both the position of the Sun and the time of day. In the morning, the Sun is in the southeast so to fly southwest, they need to keep the Sun to their left as they fly. By the afternoon, the Sun has moved to the southwest, so they need to fly toward it.

N
W E
S

Southwest

8:00 AM

4:00 PM

SUNDARBANS

Spanning Bangladesh and India, the Sundarbans is the largest mangrove forest in the world. It grows in the delta formed by three rivers as they flow into the Bay of Bengal and supports a rich variety of wildlife.

BANGLADESH

Sundarban forests

WIDE DELTA

The Sundarban delta forms where three great rivers, the Ganges, Brahmaputra, and Meghna, meet to flow into the Indian Ocean. Seen from space, the delta is revealed as a vast network of winding waterways and islands. The mangrove forest forms a dark green covering. The lighter area around the forest is densely populated agricultural land.

SALTWATER TREES

Huge mangrove forests once covered three-quarters of the world's tropical coastlines. Mangroves are tough trees that can survive a daily flooding of salty water at high tide that would kill most trees.

The mangrove trees' roots are the key to their survival. The mud they grow in is low in nutrients and the roots only extend an inch or two down. Horizontal roots form a dense mat near the surface of the mud. Vertical cone-shaped roots called pneumatophores (also known as "knees") grow up from the horizontal root system. The pneumatophores are exposed at low tide and help the roots to take in oxygen.

Bengal tigers
The Sundarban forests are home to about 200 Bengal tigers. The tigers have webbed paws and are strong swimmers, able to cover many miles at a time. They swim between the islands in the delta in search of prey such as spotted deer.

Mudskippers

Mudskippers are fish that can survive for many hours out of the water. They move along the mud by pushing themselves forward with their fins in a series of skips. When they are out of water, the mudskippers can breathe air through their skin and the lining of their mouths, but this only works while they are wet, so they have to make sure they never dry out. They hunt at low tide, eating crabs, insects, and snails, and hide away in burrows at high tide.

The **brown-winged kingfisher** only lives in tropical mangrove swamps. It feeds on crabs, shrimps, and frogs.

Largetooth sawfish patrol the shallow waters around the Sundarbans. They use their long saws to stir up the mud at the bottom and flush out prey. They will also slash the saw at groups of passing fish.

Spotted deer

Rhesus macaques are monkeys that can live in a wide range of habitats. In the Sundarbans, they hunt for snails in the mud.

FINDING A MATE

Most animals and many plants reproduce using sexual reproduction, which means that males and females need to find one another in order to mate. Animals have evolved amazing ways to make sure this happens.

Hermaphrodites
Slugs are hermaphrodites, which means that they have both male and female parts. They mate by wrapping themselves around each other and producing lots of slime.

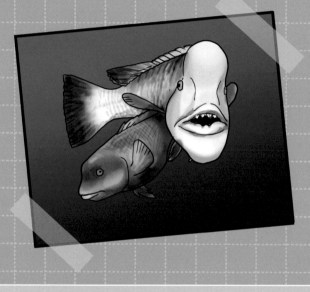

Sex-changing fish
Some species of fish change sex partway through their lives. The kobudai is a species of wrasse that lives on reefs in the Pacific Ocean. For the first 10 years of their lives, kobudai are all female, but after the age of 10, some change into males. Over the course of several months, the fish grows a bulbous forehead and chin and switches from making eggs to making sperm. The larger males are bolder and more aggressive than the females, which tend to stay hidden from view.

PERFORMING BIRDS

Birds-of-paradise live in the rain forests of New Guinea and northern Australia. The females are mostly dull brown colors. By contrast, the males grow long, multicolored feathers to impress the females and find a mate. Many, like the Vogelkop superb bird-of-paradise, clear a display area on the ground. From there, they call out to attract females. When a female arrives, the male performs a dance, showing off his amazing plumage. If the female is impressed, she will mate with him.

MIXING GENES

Many species of animals and plants use a great deal of energy to reproduce sexually. They make this effort because sexual reproduction has many advantages. By mixing the genes of two parents, sexual reproduction creates genetic variety in the offspring. This variation helps a species to survive in a changing environment as some of the offspring will be able to adapt. It also helps to protect against disease. If all offspring are genetically identical, they could all be killed by a single kind of germ.

Both the male and female grebe care for their young. This increases the chick's chances of survival.

NO MATES

Some animals that normally reproduce sexually can also reproduce without mating in a process called parthenogenesis. Female Komodo dragons, giant lizards that live on islands in Indonesia, can make offspring without mating with a male. The dragons produced by parthenogenesis are all genetically identical females. Scientists think that the dragons have evolved this ability to help them to survive in challenging times when finding a mate is hard.

CORAL REEF

Coral reefs are found in shallow seas. They are home to a rich variety of life, and a quarter of all marine animals spend part of their lives around coral reefs. The young of many fish start life there before venturing out into deeper waters. Other creatures make the reef their home for their entire lives.

Clownfish spend most of their time hiding within the tentacles of sea anemones. The anemone protects the clownfish from predators. In return, the clownfish keeps the anemone free of parasites.

The **reef shark** is the top predator on coral reefs. It feeds on fishes, octopuses, and squid.

The **Caribbean reef octopus** camouflages itself from predators such as sharks during the day. It is active at night, hunting crabs, shrimp, and fish.

Hawksbill sea turtles graze on the sponges that grow on coral reefs. The turtles help to maintain the diversity of the reef by preventing sponges from taking over from the coral.

Coral polyps are tiny creatures that form huge colonies in warm, shallow seas. They use their tentacles to capture food from the water. The polyps attach themselves to rock using a hard limestone skeleton. Over time, the skeletons of dead polyps build up to form reefs. Coral reefs are made colorful by tiny algae that live inside the polyps' soft bodies.

Packing a punch

The brilliantly colored mantis shrimp packs the strongest punch of any animal. Its clublike arm can accelerate faster than a bullet to smash open the shells of prey such as snails and crabs. The arm moves so quickly that it boils the water in front of it. This creates a bubble. When the bubble pops, it gives off a miniature explosion, which makes the punch even more destructive.

Latch

Muscles

Strong muscles pull the arm back, building up tension.

The latch releases the tension and the arm flies forward. The arm fully extends in less than 1/100 of a second.

EXTREMOPHILES

Extremophiles are organisms that can survive in extreme conditions that would be lethal to most life forms. They show how life can exist in a wide variety of environments, including those that are similar to conditions on other planets.

DEEP-SEA EXTREMES

First discovered in the 1970s, hydrothermal vents on the ocean floor are home to unique ecosystems where life does not depend on energy from the Sun. Microorganisms use chemical energy from minerals that spew from the vents. Tiny single-celled bacteria and archaea thrive in the vents, where the temperature can be more than 212°F. These extremophiles provide food for larger organisms that cluster around the vents, such as yeti crabs.

ROCK LIFE

Endoliths are extremophiles that live in rock. To cope with the scarcity of water and nutrients, bacteria inside rock can live very slowly, reproducing as rarely as once every 10,000 years. Astrobiologists study endoliths to learn what kinds of life forms may be able to survive on planets like Mars.

Nuclear-resistant

The bacterium *Deinococcus radiodurans* was discovered in 1956 by scientists running an experiment with gamma ray radiation. This hardy extremophile can survive a dose of radiation about 1,500 times stronger than a dose that would kill a human being, and it has been found living inside nuclear reactors!

LIFE UNDER THE ICE

In 2021, while drilling ice cores in the Antarctic ice sheet, geologists made a surprise discovery on a boulder under the Filchner-Ronne ice shelf. The geologists were hoping to take mud samples. Instead, they found a strange spongelike creature clinging to the boulder. How it survives down there remains a mystery.

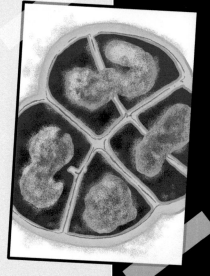

Ultimate survivor

Most extremophiles are adapted to one extreme or another, such as either heat or cold. Tardigrades are tiny animals that can survive almost any conditions. They can be frozen solid for years then come back to life when they warm up, and they can also survive boiling water. They are found in habitats ranging from deep-sea volcanic vents to the freezing cold of Antarctica. Astronauts have taken tardigrades into orbit, where they have survived both the near-vacuum of space and being bombarded with radiation.

PREDATORS AND PREY

Predators need to catch and eat prey, while prey animals try to avoid being eaten. Over time, predators have evolved weapons of attack and prey have evolved defenses against them.

FASTEST PREDATOR

Cheetahs are the fastest land animals in the world. These big cats hunt grazing mammals such as springboks on the African savanna. More than half of a cheetah's hunts are successful. However, they often have their meal stolen from them by lions, jackals, or hyenas.

When they are not being chased, springboks can often be seen pronking: jumping high in the air with straight legs. Scientists think that pronking helps individual springboks to deter predators. A springbok that can pronk very high is likely to be difficult to catch.

Cheetahs have forward-facing eyes. This gives them excellent depth perception when they are chasing prey.

Cheetahs can run at

70 mph

but they can only keep this speed up for about 1,000 feet.

The cheetah has sharp teeth, which it uses to bite through its prey's neck.

DEEP OCEAN BATTLE

Sperm whales are powerful predators that dive up to 6,000 feet in search of giant squid. The scars on the bodies of sperm whales show that the squid often fight back. The whales blast the squid with powerful sounds to stun their prey before grabbing them with their powerful teeth. The squid have a variety of defenses. They have sharp beaks and hooks on their tentacles to fight back. They can also squirt ink into the whale's face and use jet propulsion for a quick getaway.

Venomous coral snake

WARNING COLORS

Some animals defend themselves by being poisonous or venomous. Coral snakes have a venomous bite. The snakes advertise that they are venomous with bright red, yellow, and black banding on their skin. Potential predators know to keep clear. False coral snakes are non-venomous. They have a similar coloring to coral snakes in the hope that it fools predators into thinking that they are dangerous. If you look closely, you will see that there is a difference. In the southeastern USA, the bands of red on a coral snake never touch bands of black. This helps to distinguish it from the harmless milk snake.

Harmless milk snake

Springboks can run at

50 mph.

They are slower than cheetahs but can run for longer. Their best hope is to tire a cheetah out by dodging and weaving.

Springboks have eyes on the sides of their heads. This allows them to see all around them as they look out for predators.

Springboks have huge ears to help them hear a predator approaching.

GOBI DESERT

The Gobi Desert is a large desert that spans northeastern China and southern Mongolia. It has short, hot summers and long, bitterly cold winters, and the plants and animals that live there need to endure extreme conditions.

MONGOLIA

Gobi Desert

CHINA

Singing sands
The Khongoryn Els in the south of the Gobi Desert is a stretch of sand dunes 12 miles wide and 60 miles long. The largest dunes can reach 1,000 feet high. As the wind blows through the sand, it makes a loud sound that has been compared to the engine of a plane during takeoff.

WILD CAMELS

Herds of wild Bactrian camels roam long distances across the Gobi Desert in search of food and water. Unusually for mammals, wild Bactrian camels can drink salty water and they have been seen eating snow during winter.

Dense eyelashes and narrow nostrils that can close tightly protect against sandstorms.

The two humps store fat, which allows the camels to survive for months without food.

The saxaul is a small tree that is often bent into strange shapes by the wind. It has small leaves, which help it to save water in the desert.

Coat grows thick and shaggy during winter then is shed rapidly during summer.

TOP PREDATOR

Snow leopards are the top predators of the Gobi Desert. They live mostly in mountainous areas, hunting animals such as the Siberian ibex.

The **Gobi bear** is the only bear in the world that lives in deserts. It is an extremely endangered species and only about 50 bears remain in the wild.

The **bearded vulture** is a scavenger. It flies huge distances on the lookout for dead animals to eat.

The **jerboa** is a small rodent that feeds on plants and insects. It is a fast runner that can reach 15 mph. Its huge ears give it superb hearing as it listens out for predators such as the **Gobi viper**.

Wide, tough feet help with walking on sandy ground.

ISLAND LIFE

The Galápagos Islands are a group of volcanic islands that straddle the Equator in the Pacific Ocean. Isolated from the rest of the world, many species of animals and plants on the islands are found nowhere else.

Galápagos
Islands

ECUADOR

COLD WATERS

The Galápagos Islands sit in the Humboldt Current, an ocean current that brings cold water up from the Antarctic. As a result, the water temperature stays below 77°F all year. Many fish thrive in these relatively cool waters, feeding on tiny plants called phytoplankton. In turn, the fish provide food for animals such as the Galápagos sea lion and the Galápagos penguin, the only penguin that lives this far north.

GIANT TORTOISES

Weighing up to 880 pounds, the Galápagos giant tortoise is the largest tortoise in the world. There are 12 species of tortoise spread over ten islands. These tough reptiles feed on grass, fruit, and cactus pads, but they can survive for up to a year without water or food. They can live for more than 100 years.

Finches are often seen on the backs of giant tortoises. They eat ticks from the tortoises' skin.

Galápagos
penguins

Galápagos
sea lions

INSPIRING DARWIN

Charles Darwin visited the Galápagos Islands as part of a scientific expedition in 1835.

Darwin collected samples of the animals he found on the islands. He later studied the samples and realized that species on the different islands were related to one another. Each species had evolved to suit the habitats found on its island. For example, finches had differently shaped beaks depending on their diet.

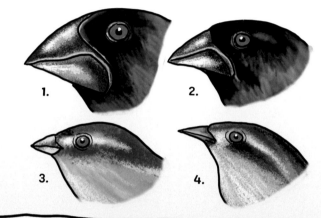

1.

2.

3.

4.

1. The large ground finch feeds on hard nuts and seeds.
2. The medium ground finch feeds on seeds.
3. The small tree finch feeds on insects.
4. The green warbler finch feeds on small insects.

Unique plants

Out of the 552 species of plants found on the Galápagos Islands, 180 of them are found nowhere else in the world. These include Scalesia, small trees that grow in dense forests in the wetter parts of the islands.

OCEAN LIZARD

The marine iguana is the only lizard in the world that forages in the sea. The iguanas can spend up to an hour at a time underwater, feeding on algae. When they emerge from the cool water, they warm themselves up again by lying on warm rocks, basking in the sun.

HUMANS AND THE NATURAL WORLD

The last mass extinction event, which wiped out the dinosaurs, took place on our planet 66 million years ago. Scientists warn that we are now experiencing another one due to the way humans are changing the planet. We need to act quickly to preserve the diverse ecosystems found on Earth.

HOW MANY SPECIES ARE WE LOSING?

Nobody knows how many species of life there are on Earth. Scientists estimate that there may be as many as 100 million different species. Many scientists think that more than 10,000 species are becoming extinct each year, a rate that has increased by more than 1,000 times due to human activity!

The once-common Javan rhino is close to extinction due to hunting and habitat loss. Just 75 individuals are left in the wild, living on the Indonesian island of Java.

Climate change

Over recent decades, human activity has caused global warming. This has placed many ecosystems in danger. Coral reefs (see pages 34–35) are threatened by rising ocean temperatures. Coral thrives in warm, salty water between 73°–84° Fahrenheit. However, if the temperature rises above 86°F for a prolonged period, the polyps expel the algae from inside their bodies and the reef turns white. This is called bleaching. Coral can recover from bleaching, but if the water remains hot for too long, it can kill the reef.

WHAT CAN WE DO?

The major cause of global warming is the burning of fossil fuels such as oil. We need to dramatically reduce the amount of fossil fuels we burn, switching over to renewable sources of energy such as wind and solar. We can also help by using our cars less and riding our bicycles more! All around the world, groups of people are coming together to plant trees. The Plant to Stop Poverty group organizes communities in countries such as Tanzania to help them to restore forests. The group has so far planted more than 150,000 trees.

You can help to preserve species by volunteering at a local nature center or wildlife refuge. Many organizations run projects to survey local wildlife, such as counting the birds that visit your back yard. This takes patience, but it will improve your observational skills!

Habitat destruction

Many habitats are destroyed to make way for cities, industry, or farmland. In the last 200 years, two-thirds of the world's rainforests have been cut down and turned into farmland. This results in soils losing their nutrients and has led to the extinction of many species. In Brazil, 20 percent of the rainforest has disappeared since the 1970s.

GRETA THUNBERG

Swedish environmental activist Greta Thunberg (born 2003) shot to global attention in 2018 when, at the age of just 15, she skipped school to stand outside the Swedish parliament building and call for greater action on climate change. Thunberg's actions inspired thousands of schoolchildren around the world to begin similar campaigns.

GLOSSARY

bacteria
Tiny single-celled organisms that measure just a few millionths of a millimeter in length.

biome
An area with the physical conditions suitable for a particular group of plants, animals, and other organisms to live there.

camouflage
The way in which animals or other organisms remain hidden from others by blending in with their background or having a coloring that breaks up their shape.

coral
A rocklike substance formed in shallow oceans by the skeletal remains of tiny creatures called polyps. Over time, the remains build up to form coral reefs.

delta
A wetland area that forms where a river spreads out and empties into the oceans or a lake.

digestion
The breaking down of food inside the body.

ecosystem
A particular physical environment and all the organisms that live within it.

evolution
The process by which species change into new species over time. Evolution is a gradual process that takes place over many generations.

exoskeleton
A hard external layer that protects and supports the bodies of invertebrates such as insects.

extinction
The disappearance of a whole species of organism.

fungus
A group of spore-producing organisms that feed on decaying material or other organisms. Fungi include yeasts, molds, and mushrooms.

hydrothermal vent
An opening on the ocean floor out of which hot, mineral-rich water flows. The energy and minerals from hydrothermal vents support many different life forms.

larva
The young of invertebrate animals such as insects or crustaceans.

microorganism
A tiny organism that is too small to see with the naked eye.

migration
The seasonal movement of animals from one part of the world to another.

organism
An individual life form, such as an animal, plant, fungus, or bacterium.

parthenogenesis
Reproduction from an unfertilized egg.

photosynthesis
The chemical process by which plants and some other organisms use the energy of the sun to make nutrients from carbon dioxide and water.

phytoplankton
Tiny organisms such as green algae that live in the sea and photosynthesize.

predator
An animal that hunts and eats other animals.

rain forest
A dense forest rich in life that grows in areas with high levels of rainfall.

reproduction
The process by which organisms produce offspring. Reproduction is a feature common to all life forms.

species
A group of similar organisms that are able to reproduce with one another and produce fertile offspring.

tendon
A flexible, strong cord that attaches a muscle to a bone in the bodies of animals.

venom
A toxic substance produced by the bodies of some animals. The animals inject venom into other animals as a means of capturing prey or as a defense against predators.

vertebrate
An animal with a backbone, such as a mammal, a bird, or a fish. Animals without a backbone are called invertebrates.

INDEX